Military Animals

MILITARY ANIMAL
MASCOTS

by Ryan Gale

DiscoverRoo
An Imprint of Pop!
booksonline.com

abdobooks.com

Published by Pop!, a division of ABDO, PO Box 398166, Minneapolis, Minnesota 55439. Copyright ©2022 by Abdo Consulting Group, Inc. International copyrights reserved in all countries. No part of this book may be reproduced in any form without written permission from the publisher. DiscoverRoo™ is a trademark and logo of Pop!.

Printed in the United States of America, North Mankato, Minnesota.

102021
012022

THIS BOOK CONTAINS RECYCLED MATERIALS

Cover Photo: US Department of Defense
Interior Photos: US Department of Defense, 1; Defense Visual Information Distribution Service, 5, 6, 8, 9, 17 (top), 19, 20, 23, 26–27, 28 (left), 28 (right); Konrad Giehr/picture-alliance/dpa/AP Images, 11; North Wind Picture Archives, 12; Library of Congress, 13; The Print Collector/Alamy, 15; iStockphoto, 16, 17 (bottom); Jane Barlow/PA Wire/PA Wire URN:28447301/Press Association/AP Images, 25

Editor: Charly Haley
Series Designer: Laura Graphenteen
Library of Congress Control Number: 2020948855
Publisher's Cataloging-in-Publication Data
Names: Gale, Ryan, author.
Title: Military animal mascots / by Ryan Gale
Description: Minneapolis, Minnesota : Pop!, 2022 | Series: Military animals | Includes online resources and index.
Identifiers: ISBN 9781532169953 (lib. bdg.) | ISBN 9781644945902 (pbk.) | ISBN 9781098240882 (ebook)
Subjects: LCSH: Animals--Juvenile literature. | Working animals--Juvenile literature. | Mascots--Juvenile literature. | Armed Forces--Juvenile literature.
Classification: DDC 355.424--dc23

WELCOME TO DiscoverRoo!

Pop open this book and you'll find QR codes loaded with information, so you can learn even more!

Scan this code* and others like it while you read, or visit the website below to make this book pop!

popbooksonline.com/mascots

*Scanning QR codes requires a web-enabled smart device with a QR code reader app and a camera.

TABLE OF CONTENTS

CHAPTER 1

CHESTY THE DOG

A spotlight shines on a US **marine**. He is

at a military base in Washington, DC.

A bulldog sits by his side. The dog wears

a military uniform. The marine speaks

to a large group of visitors. He tells them

WATCH A VIDEO HERE!

the dog's name is Chesty. The dog is

the base's mascot. Chesty and the

marine are part

of a military parade

at the base.

Marines march

in the parade.

A military band

plays music.

Chesty the bulldog represents marines at different events.

One US Army unit has both a donkey mascot and a goat mascot.

Some military animal mascots are symbols of strength. They are meant to **inspire** soldiers. Some are symbols of things from the past. They remind soldiers of the military's history. Others are symbols of home. They remind soldiers of where they come from. Some mascots are thought to bring good luck.

DID YOU KNOW?

Mascot is a French word meaning "good luck charm."

Animals are chosen as military mascots for many reasons. Some animals have **traits** that soldiers like. Bulldogs, for example, are tough.

The US Marine Corps has had many bulldogs named Chesty.

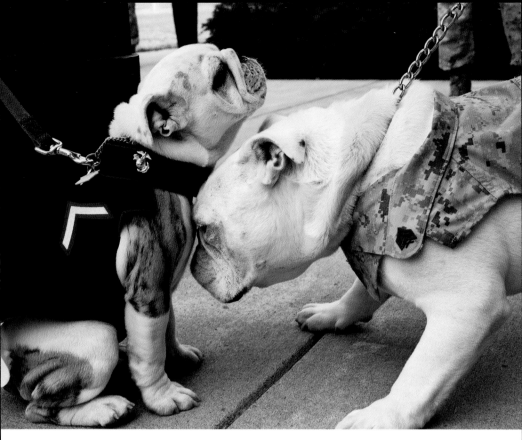

US marines have had bulldog mascots since 1922.

Animals from certain places are also chosen. Soldiers sometimes find homeless animals. They adopt them. Some of these animals become mascots.

CHAPTER 2

HISTORY OF MILITARY MASCOTS

Militaries have had animal mascots for more than 2,000 years. One of the first known mascots was a pair of **vultures**. They were used by an **ancient** Roman army.

LEARN MORE HERE!

Military animal mascots became popular in Great Britain in the 1770s. The US military began using them in the 1800s.

A British Army unit had a goat named Taffy as its mascot in 1961.

Some animal mascots have been carried into battle. They **inspired** soldiers. Old Abe was a bald eagle. He was a mascot during the American Civil War (1861–1865). He sat on a wooden pole.

Old Abe served with a US Army unit from Wisconsin during the Civil War.

A statue at the Vicksburg National Military Park in Mississippi honors Old Abe.

The pole was carried by a soldier.

Old Abe was trained to open his wings

on command. He was in more than

30 battles.

Many World War I (1914–1918) pilots had animal mascots. Some pilots even brought their dogs while they flew missions. They thought the mascots would bring them good luck.

Sometimes soldiers adopt pets or mascots. A US **marine** in Iraq adopted

DID YOU KNOW?

The US Navy had a pig mascot named King Neptune in World War II (1939–1945). The mascot got people's attention and helped raise money for the war. It helped raise more than $19 million.

A couple of dogs sit with a group of British military pilots in 1914.

a donkey in 2008. He made it a mascot.

Then, he had the donkey shipped to the

United States in 2011. The donkey lived

with him after he retired.

TIMELINE

1861

A bald eagle named Old Abe becomes the mascot of a military unit during the American Civil War.

1770s

Animal mascots become popular in the British military.

1914–1918

Animal mascots are used by military pilots during World War I.

1922

A bulldog becomes the mascot of the US Marine Corps.

1972

A military unit in Norway makes a king penguin its mascot.

2008

A US marine in Iraq adopts a donkey as a mascot.

CHAPTER 3

MILITARY MASCOT JOBS

Some animal mascots are used in special events. They take part in military parades. These parades are done to display military skills, such as marching. Mascots are also used in military sporting events.

COMPLETE AN ACTIVITY HERE!

Soldiers greet their mascot at a military ceremony.

Therapy dogs are trained to be calm as they comfort soldiers and other people.

Some military animal mascots work as **therapy** animals. They visit soldiers in military bases and hospitals. They help soldiers feel less stressed.

Some military mascots are pets. They provide friendship and comfort to military members and their families.

Animals may need training before becoming mascots. Dogs often need to learn **obedience**. Some animals may need to get used to being around people.

Military animal **handlers** also need training. They need to learn what foods their animals can eat. They need to know how to cut the animals' hair and trim their nails. They may also need to know how to dress their mascots.

DID YOU KNOW?

Military animal mascots retire when they get old. They are often replaced with other animals that look like them.

Harry the dog is the mascot at a US Coast Guard station in New York City.

CHAPTER 4

MILITARY ANIMAL MASCOTS TODAY

Animal mascots are found in militaries around the world. Many kinds of animals are used as mascots. Dogs and goats are popular in the United Kingdom and the United States. A military unit in Norway

LEARN MORE HERE!

has a king penguin. One in Sri Lanka has an elephant mascot. Another in Croatia has a tiger. Militaries from many countries use horses, donkeys, and mules as mascots.

Nils Olav is a king penguin. He serves as a mascot for a military unit in Norway.

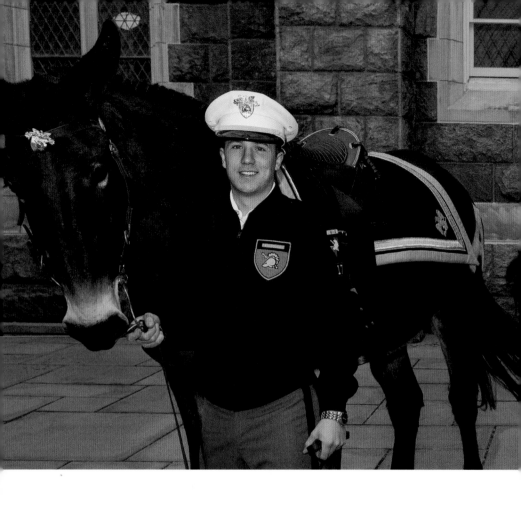

Mascots often live in kennels or stables at military bases. Some live at zoos. Mascots have to stay behind

The US Army has mule mascots that live at West Point, which is an army training school.

when soldiers work overseas. Mascots

that are owned by military units have

handlers to take care of them.

MASCOT UNIFORMS

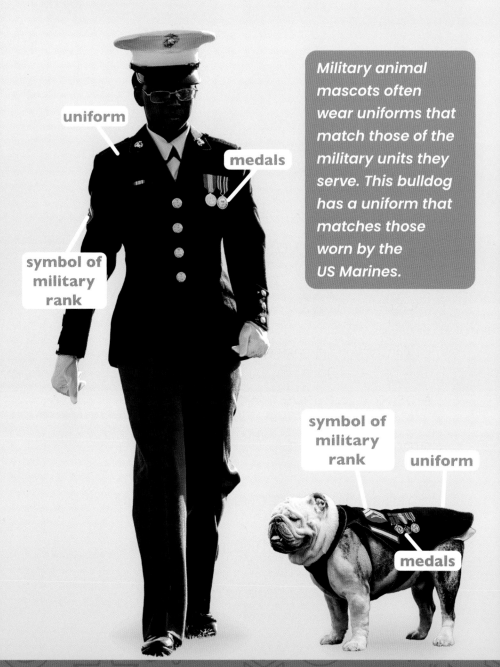

uniform

medals

symbol of
military
rank

Military animal mascots often wear uniforms that match those of the military units they serve. This bulldog has a uniform that matches those worn by the US Marines.

symbol of
military
rank

uniform

medals

Military mascots often wear uniforms.

Some uniforms are for everyday use.

Others are only worn for special events.

A uniform may show the mascot's name

or a symbol of its military **rank**.

Many kinds of animals are military

mascots. They can remind people

of history and make people happy.

Mascots continue to serve militaries

around the world.

DID YOU KNOW? Sometimes mascots earn medals. They wear the medals on their uniforms.

MAKING CONNECTIONS

TEXT-TO-SELF

Have you ever seen an animal mascot? Was it for the military or something else? What animal was it? What was the animal doing?

TEXT-TO-TEXT

Have you read other books about military animals? How were the animals in those books similar to or different from the ones in this book?

TEXT-TO-WORLD

Militaries around the world have different animals as mascots. What animal would be a good mascot for the place you live?

GLOSSARY

ancient — from a long time ago.

handler — a person who is in charge of a military animal.

inspire — to motivate somebody.

marine — a member of the US Marine Corps, which is part of the US military.

obedience — the act of following rules or doing what a person says.

rank — a military member's level of service.

therapy — a form of medical treatment, often for mental health.

trait — the way something looks or acts.

vulture — a type of large bird.

INDEX

ONLINE RESOURCES

popbooksonline.com

Scan this code* and others like it while you read, or visit the website below to make this book pop!

popbooksonline.com/mascots

*Scanning QR codes requires a web-enabled smart device with a QR code reader app and a camera.